GOOD THINGS

COME TO THOSE WHO ~~WAIT~~ TAKE*

*Taking hold of all that God has for your life

DONNY KARPINEN

Contents

Foreword

I'm very excited about Pastor Donny's new book. As a Pastor and Life Coach for over 30 years I have seen so many people come so close to their own personal finish line and never quite finish the race. In his new book Pastor Donny explains that every one of us has wonderful promises from God. We must secondly understand and walk out the principles in order for the promise to even have a chance. Where this new book gets the attention of the reader is when he teaches us step by step how to get through the problems that we face before we enter into the promise land. In my profession I deal with so many amazing individuals who have wonderful promises but they lack the skills, tools, and attitude to apprehend what is rightfully theirs. Thank you Pastor Donny for being a wonderful example who understands the pain, price, and also the privilege of being everything that God has called us to be.

- Tim Storey

Introduction

"God will never give you more than you can handle."

"God only helps those who help themselves."

"Good things come to those who wait."

What do these phrases all have in common? They aren't in the Bible. They sound like they might be, but I assure you they are not. The saying "Good things come to those who wait" is just an old English proverb, and while it is an acceptable principle, it is not a Bible scripture. In at least some senses, the Bible directly contradicts this very idea, and I want to present you with a different view: "Good things come to those who take."

Now, the Bible's writers seem to agree with the values of patience and endurance. I am not writing to counteract the importance of patience and long-suffering as we endure trials, entirely relying on God. These are even two of the Fruits of the Spirit listed in the New Testament! I want to argue that a closer examination of the Kingdom of God requires a passionate "taking hold of" and not a passive "waiting for" things to come to me.

Jesus said,

> "And from the days of John the Baptist until now, the kingdom of heaven suffers violence, and the violent **take it** by force."
>
> Matthew 11:12

Jesus was not implying that there is an assault on Heaven, the Kingdom of God, or even Himself in a negative sense. The Savior was expressing desperation in people for the Truth. People were desperate for the Kingdom of God and all the freedom and healing it brings.

Imagine those internet videos of people rushing the stores for Black Friday sales, trampling each other, and acting like the apocalypse is happening. Yet, instead of commercialism, this is a desperation in people's souls we're talking about. Instead of people panicking at not getting 40% off that new PS5, these are people flipping out over the assurance of abundance for their souls!

Think about it. Multitudes of people followed Jesus to hear Him speak (Matthew 14:13- 21). Some followers even cut a hole in the roof of a building and lowered a paralyzed man into it in hopes that Jesus would heal him (Mark 2:3-5). The woman with "the issue of blood" broke the ceremonial law by being out in public because she was desperate to touch a piece of His clothing (Luke 8:43-48). The Bible often refers to them as a "throng" of people. Scholars say "throng" means the people pressing their bodies into anyone they could to get a glimpse of Him. They were going crazier than teenage girls at a Jonas Brothers concert!

Like Black Friday's rabid consumers, people desperately thronged Jesus for access to the Kingdom. Whether we can recognize it or not, that same desperation is still in us today. And this is a good desperation. The Bible says God has placed "eternity" in the hearts of men (Ecclesiastes 3:11). I firmly believe that this feeling is about far more than just salvation! I am committed to every person coming into the restoration of their birthright. This birthright is not about being a victim of circumstances or just "getting by." It is about the gift of having dominion and subduing the earth. Our birthright is the gift to rule and reign with Christ! That blessing is ultimately what this book is all about.

Friends, Christianity is bigger than forgiveness for our sins. This principle is more significant than going to church on Sundays. This idea is more important than merely reading your Bible. I'm talking about total redemption. I'm talking about taking hold of eternal life and the Kingdom of God today, not just after death.

In the words of John Foreman, "And I wonder why would I wait till I die to come alive? I'm ready now. I'm not waiting for the afterlife."

Whether you are a seeker, a brand new Christian, a pastor, or someone that has been following Jesus for decades, I pray these chapters open your eyes to see that there is more for all of us, and it is ours for the taking.

Taking Hold of
Your Design

God's plan for humanity is bigger than the forgiveness of our sins.

If you've grown up in church like me, you may think that that's a bold statement. Did I say something blasphemous? Did I trivialize Jesus' sacrifice on the cross? I don't think so at all. Let me explain.

Growing up, I was morbidly aware of my childhood sins and shortcomings. I would live in a perpetual state of fear that God's judgment would rain down on me for any little wrong thing I had done or even for intrusive thoughts I had in my mind. At that time, I did not doubt God's existence, but I lacked a complete understanding of His love, grace, mercy, and blessed assurance of salvation. I'm still not sure which "sinner's prayer" actually "took," but one thing was for sure. I was a child of God who desperately needed a greater revelation of the Agape love of the Father.

As a result, in my mind, a Christian "witnessing" to others might look something like this:

Christian:	*"Did you know that God loves you and has a plan for your life even though you are complete scum?"*
Other person:	*"What? That's an odd thing to say."*
Christian:	*"Yeah, it's true. God created you, but you suck in every way, and you need to be forgiven. That's God's whole plan! He came down out of Heaven to forgive you! Isn't that amazing?!"*

Other person: *"Wow, this feels a bit rude and aggressive. It doesn't feel loving or caring, but a part of me wants to know if there really is a God. But what if I don't believe you?"*

Christian: *"Unfortunately, you'll burn in hell forever and be tortured for all of eternity."*

Other person: *"WHAT?! Well, I guess when I think about it, I definitely do think I suck. I mean, I did do that one thing. And I still do some of these other things. But you're saying I can be forgiven for everything I have done?"*

Christian: *"Yes! You have a choice! Pray this prayer and be forgiven, then you can live in paradise with the world's most delectable food, streets of gold, and the most beautiful beaches, and enjoy absolute peace forever... or experience eternal torment. You can choose right now!"*

Other person: *"Uhh, well, if this is true, let's go with the opposite of eternal torment..."*

When it comes to witnessing, I do not recommend this method. I am certainly not saying that Heaven and hell do not exist. What I am saying is that we cannot scare people into Heaven. The most compelling thing about Heaven should be that God is there. God's beauty, holiness, and unconditional love are the attractors. It's more precious than anything else in all creation.

When we talk about Heaven, it's the New Heavens and the New Earth that we're talking about (Revelation 21:1). God will establish His Kingdom here on earth and "reset" it to His original design, just like in the Garden of Eden. And this leads us to God's plan of redemption. It *includes* forgiveness, but it is not *limited* to it.

God is a God of redemption. That's His big plan. He loves to redeem people (Galatians 4:4-5).

To redeem something is to "purchase back; to ransom."

Additionally, to "ransom" someone or something is "to obtain the release of (a prisoner) by making a payment demanded."

In this case, what had to be "purchased back?" Redemption was the original intent of humanity's grand design. **God's original design for us was to rule and reign. God created us to subdue the earth and have dominion.** This assertion can seem foreign even to many Christians, but it shouldn't.

The Bible speaks this truth throughout its pages, especially in the very first chapter of the Bible: the book of Genesis.

> And God said, Let us make man in our image, after our likeness: and let them have dominion over the fish of the sea, and over the fowl of the air, and over the cattle, and over all the earth, and over every creeping thing that creepeth upon the earth. So God created man in his own image, in the image of God created he him; male and female created he them. And God blessed them, and God said unto them, Be fruitful, and multiply, and replenish the earth, **and subdue it: and have dominion** over the fish of the sea, and over the fowl of the air, and over every living thing that moveth upon the earth.
>
> Genesis 1:26-28 KJV

His instructions were to subdue the earth and take dominion.

When God created Adam and Eve in His image, He graciously gave them authority, just like He had to rule over His creation.

After that, something awful happened.

When Adam and Eve rebelled against God, not only did sin enter the world and bring decay and separation of the perfect intimacy they once had with God, but something more was lost: the Holy Spirit living in them.

> And the Lord God formed man of the dust of the ground, and breathed into his nostrils the breath of life; and man became a living being.
>
> Genesis 2:7

> And the Lord God commanded the man, saying, "You may surely eat of every tree of the garden, but of the tree of the knowledge of good and evil you shall not eat, for in the day that you eat of it you shall surely die."
>
> Genesis 2:16-17

But they didn't *actually* die that day, did they? So what happened?

The Holy Spirit living in them no longer dwelled within them as He once did. As a result, they were no longer immortal, but decay began to set in. For the first time, their lives had expiration dates.

The Old Testament references the Holy Spirit *coming upon* people for remarkable feats, displays of power, and purposes of glorifying God. Yet it doesn't say anything about the Holy Spirit *living within* people again until after Jesus' resurrection and the promised Holy Spirit coming on the day of Pentecost.

God's original design for us was to rule and reign. God created us to subdue the earth and have dominion.

This is the reason Jesus said to the disciples that it was "to their advantage" that He would go away so that The Comforter (Holy Spirit) could come (John 14:16).

And the most amazing thing has happened!

God's presence could no longer be contained in a temple or a tabernacle, but He would now dwell within human hearts again.

This beautiful truth should give us enormous self-respect when considering God Himself has chosen to dwell within us.

It is almost impossible for us to fully conceive.

As I write this chapter, I am gazing at the glorious Montana skies and thinking about the wonder of this reality.

Take a moment to think about how remarkable this is.

The Creator of the universe.
The One who made the oceans.
The Grand Canyon and Niagara Falls.
These glorious Montana skies.
He lives inside of you.

This reality moves me to awe and tears. It should stir something up within each of us. The list of things we can feel is endless: Gratitude. Confidence. Humility. Purpose.

God's presence could no longer be contained in a temple or a tabernacle, but He would now dwell within human hearts again. This beautiful truth should give us enormous self-respect when considering God Himself has chosen to dwell within us.

The intent of this book is not just to point out big spiritual truths and grandiose concepts. I am more concerned about what we do with these truths to make a difference in our lives and the world than merely offering more knowledge to keep in our heads. The central theme of this book is ultimately about purpose.

Jesus purchased back our right to rule and reign with Him, and He gave us the Holy Spirit again.

Forgiveness of our sins is necessary, but it is not the end. It is part of the means to an end.

God is restoring our future to His original design so we can operate in our purpose with Him. God's plan of redemption includes forgiveness but is not limited to it.

As our hearts and minds open to this bigger picture, I pray that it stirs up holy awe, wonder, a sense of purpose, and desire for more than what you have been experiencing in your life thus far.

God made us to be more. We were made for more.

Not only are you loved unconditionally, forgiven, and free, but your birthright to rulership has been redeemed!

Taking On The "one" Who Hates You

I was born
into the world
through
warfare.

Before I was born, there was a battle for my life.

When my mom was pregnant with me in 1989, she began having complications just seven weeks into the pregnancy. She had all the symptoms of a miscarriage, and the doctors informed her that she had almost certainly lost the baby.

They decided to do an ultrasound the following day, and if there were no signs of a heartbeat, it would officially be declared a miscarriage. Two important things happened that night.

The first is that my mom called another Christian woman for encouragement and prayer. Shockingly, she received the opposite of what she had hoped.

My mom remembers the woman not encouraging her to have any faith but instead to prepare for the worst.

I'm sure she meant well, but this call was incredibly discouraging. My story wasn't over, but she was acting like it already was! Sadly, many Christians do not believe in God for the impossible, ask Him for the impossible, or work with Him in faith for supernatural breakthroughs.

That same night, however, my dad battled in the spiritual realm. He prayed, and he declared healing. By faith, he contended for a miracle. He had a vision that he was fighting a dragon with a sword and shield.

He recalls fighting and warring until he was utterly exhausted. The next thing he saw was his sword lowered, but the dragon was dead underneath another warrior's feet. While my dad was exhausted from the fight, Jesus came and finished the battle.

The following day, the doctors performed an ultrasound, and my tiny heart was still beating. On January 11th, 1990, I was born healthy and whole.

There has always been a call of God on my life to preach, and the Spirit of the Lord is upon me to join with Jesus and proclaim *"good news to the poor, liberty to the captives, recovery of sight to the blind, and to free those who are oppressed"* (Luke 4:18).

And because 1 Corinthians 6:17 tells me that *"the person who is joined to the Lord is one spirit with Him,"* I know I am a threat to satan's kingdom.

One of the greatest truths of the Bible is that we are overcomers. The Scriptures even tell us that we are more than conquerors (Romans 8:37).

But the question we must ask ourselves is this: "What (or who) do we overcome?"

Leading question. The answer is satan.

Not everyone is willing to admit this, but the Bible gives us plenty of evidence that satan is the one who hates us. (Ephesians 2:2; 2 Corinthians 11:3)

Before earthly time began, satan was seated in heavenly places and enjoying the wonders of Heaven. He was an angelic being, but he was kicked out of Heaven when he rebelled against God and contended for His glory. In the future, we believe that a lake of fire awaits him, his demons, and fellow fallen angels that followed his rebellion.

Why? Because satan hates God. But satan also hates you because God has created you in His image.

Many people like to bury their heads in the sand and believe that the world is a better place than it is. And yes, the earth has some unmistakably profound beauty.

We can see breathtaking sunrises, sunsets, waterfalls, canyons, and countryside. When we genuinely enjoy nature, we taste Eden and the new world to come. While this is refreshing and restorative to our souls, it is also true that satan has a limited right to rule the earth and is wreaking havoc on humanity at this point in history. (1 John 5:19; 2 Corinthians 4:4).

When Jesus was 30, John the Baptist baptized Him into His public ministry. When Jesus emerged from the water, the Holy Spirit descended like a dove and rested on Him.

At the same time, God the Father from Heaven declared, *"This is my beloved Son, with whom I am well pleased"* (John 3:17 ESV). What would you have expected would happen next? Immediately after receiving heavenly approval, most would assume that Jesus would have started traveling, speaking, and healing.

But this is not the way in the Kingdom of God.

Instantly after being baptized, the Bible tells us that the Holy Spirit led Jesus out to the wilderness to be tempted by satan (Matthew 4:1). In the wilderness, Jesus was fasting for 40 days and 40 nights, and He had a face-off with satan.

The evil adversary tempted Him three different times, but the third temptation was sobering and eye-opening. For the third temptation, satan takes Jesus to a high mountain and shows Him "all the kingdoms of the world and their glory." He offered them to Jesus for a price: He would only have to bow down and worship him. Of course, Jesus refuses satan by quoting Scripture, but He does not argue that the kingdoms are under satan's authority to give.

This dramatic incident took place before Jesus performed a single miracle. The temptations took place even before Jesus started preaching. Satan knew the threat to his kingdom of darkness and wanted to eliminate Jesus' ministry before it began.

In the same way, satan wants to take out the children of God before we can get started in our purpose. If he can tempt us before we have a track record of seeing God's goodness and glory, he can weaken our spirits for the battle. **Our power comes from a track record of victories from God's strength. That gives us the confidence to face down the devil again and again in the present and the future.**

The enemy has tried to take me out of the battle in many ways. He did some significant damage to me and my family when I was 25 years old, questioning whether I would become a Lead Pastor. I can now see that this was a demonic attack against my destiny to succeed my dad as Lead Pastor of Victory Church, the church he founded.

Notice that the attack was long before I stepped into the authority of lead pastoring Victory. I succeeded my dad on June 6th, 2021, on the church's 25th anniversary when I was 31. At 25, I didn't know if I would ever see the day.

Satan will continue to attack. Luke's account of Jesus' temptation in the wilderness tells us it wasn't over when Jesus successfully resisted satan's three temptations.

"And when the devil had ended every temptation, he departed from him until an opportune time." (Luke 4:13 ESV) So satan will continue to try, but I will continue to triumph over him.

Our power comes from a track record of victories from God's strength. That gives us the confidence to face down the devil again and again in the present and the future.

I'm not anxious about what lies ahead because I see God continuing to protect His promises over my life. I see His faithfulness in the past, so I'm confident of His faithfulness in the future.

Today, I agree with my friend Ben Courson when he says, "I used to be afraid of the dark, but now the dark is afraid of me."

Satan doesn't just hate me. He hates you too.

Jesus warned us: *"The thief comes only to steal and kill and destroy; I have come that they may have life, and have it to the full"* (John 10:10 NIV).

So there it is; satan's main objective is to destroy, discourage, and take us out of the game. He desires to make you hate your life and question God's love for you. Many have been convinced that their "belovedness" to God is based upon their behavior, goodness, or accomplishments.

I want to remind you that the Father spoke belovedness over Jesus before He started His public ministry and before He accomplished a single thing. The same is true for you and me. We are loved because God is love (1 John 4:16). We are loved because we were created in the image of God, and before we were formed in our mother's wombs, He knew us (Jeremiah 1:5).

Just as Jesus was a threat to satan's reign, so are the children of God that carry the Holy Spirit. The same power that raised Jesus from the dead lives in you! (Romans 6:10-11).

Satan hates that! Furthermore, he's terrified of it. He attacks you because he's afraid of you.

If you are under attack, have you considered that it's not because something is wrong with you but because something is right with you?

If you aren't experiencing opposition from satan and his kingdom of darkness, perhaps it's because you've been playing in a way that's consistent with his team. If you are no threat, then you'll experience no attack.

Satan's time is limited. Ultimately, God's plan is for Jesus to return one final time and reset the world as He initially dreamt and created it, like in the Garden of Eden. God will destroy satan, exclusively rule and reign the New Heavens and Earth, and those in Christ will rule and reign with Jesus forever. (2 Timothy 2:12; Daniel 7:18).

They will laugh, feast, worship, and dance in His victory. The Bible says, *"And they overcame him by the blood of the Lamb and by the word of their testimony"* (Revelation 12:11a). This promise is for everyone in Christ and sealed by the blood of Jesus shed on Calvary.

What I love about God's heart is that He wants as many people to join Him in this victory over satan as possible (2 Peter 3:9).

We believe God will send Jesus one last time to initiate the consummation of the current earth and the new world, the final death blow to satan and his evil army. It's important to note that the only thing that God is waiting for is that more people will come to know Him.

He is patient, more patient than we can comprehend. *"And count the patience of our Lord as salvation, just as our beloved brother Paul also wrote to you according to the wisdom given him"* (2 Peter 3:15). His patience is for salvation, for more people to accept His gift of salvation.

Can I ask you a question before I go any further in this book?

Have you received Jesus' sacrifice for you?

Have you invited the Holy Spirit to live within you, make you new, and wash you clean of your sin?

This gift of salvation is not specially reserved for the "good people." It is not reserved for the people who have perfect attendance in church. This gift is available to anyone who wants it. God's arms are always open wide. He is kinder than you think He is, and He is more patient with you than you are with yourself.

If you are under attack, have you considered that it's not because something is wrong with you but because something is right with you?

No one can be "scared into heaven" by being terrified of a place called hell.

The Holy Spirit draws people to Himself through His perfect love. He doesn't use fear. The most terrifying thing when I think about the concept of hell isn't the "Dante's Inferno" depiction, but it's simply the fact that God isn't there.

If God isn't there, love isn't there. If love isn't there, life isn't there. This truth means God's love is even better than life (Psalm 63).

If you'd like to receive Jesus' gift of salvation, you only have to accept it. Reject fear; embrace love. God hasn't given you a spirit of fear but power, love, and a sound mind (2 Timothy 1:7). See His kindness and patience. See His holiness and recognize that you can trade your sin for His righteousness. You can do that right now if you want to receive it and be called righteous. Let me lead you in this prayer, and I'd encourage you to pray it out loud:

> *"God, thank You for loving me. Thank You for creating me in Your image. Thank You for reconciling me through Your Son, Jesus. I receive His life for my life. I receive His purification of my sins. I am a new creation. God, from this day forward, You are my Father, and I am Your child. I love You. Amen."*

If you just prayed that prayer or have already prayed something similar and received Jesus' salvation, I rejoice with you!

In many ways, this is where the battle begins, not ends. The eternal security of your salvation is not in question, but your heart and mind will be under attack until either you die or Jesus returns because now you've enlisted in the army. If you are a member of God's Kingdom army and marvelous light, you are His ambassador (2 Corinthians 5:20).

There is a target on your back, but take heart, for you will overcome it.

On the cross, Jesus said, "It is finished." He was speaking of the work done to reconcile man to God, to relocate the presence of God again to human hearts, and to enable us to triumph over the one who hates us.

Taking
Responsibility

The trauma that affected my grandmother affected my mother. Now, that trauma also affects me.

When I was in elementary school, I suffered from debilitating fear. Of course, I did not know why I felt this way or what to call it at the time, but hindsight has given me language for what I was experiencing.

When my parent's car pulled up to drop me off at Westminster Academy, my mind would start an invisible countdown. But this timer was not like the other kids in my school. While they were counting down the hours until school was out, I was dreading pickup time. For some reason that I still cannot explain, I was terrified that no one would pick me up.

There was a visceral fear of abandonment and isolation that plagued me during every class period. While my classmates were having fun during recess, I would take glances at the after-school pickup area, dreading when school would dismiss. While the teacher would attempt to educate us, my brain would not process anything she was saying. I was convinced, without any evidence, that when I walked out of school, no one would be there.

Eventually, my dad adjusted his pickup strategy to alleviate my fears. He would arrive at the school 30 minutes earlier than the pickup time, park far away, and walk to my classroom door. He would stand right outside the small rectangular window in the door where I could see him. After I finally saw his face in the window, I could take a breath and listen to what the teacher was saying.

Until I saw his face, I couldn't stop looking at the clock.

The door.

The clock.

The door.

The clock.

The moment I saw him, my fears were relieved. I never had the language to understand that my fears were a manifestation of anxiety. The conversation around mental health was not as popular then as it is now, and I'm thankful for therapy.

I understand as much as anyone else that mental health struggles are real. These struggles, illnesses, and challenges result from a broken world needing redemption.

With satan's limited right to the earth, the world is not how it should be.

It is not how God envisioned when He made the Garden of Eden. More importantly, this is not how it will be at the renewal of all things. **Remember, God's plan is bigger than forgiveness. It's redemption.**

With the world in its current fallen state, there is anxiety, pain, trauma, betrayal, death, disease, and depression. It touches everyone. When sin entered the world, all of these things that are detrimental to the human experience entered it, and there was no escaping them. Yet, we have hope, and we press on.

For some Christians, the struggle of living in a fallen world is so simply accepted that they can unknowingly adopt a victim mentality, a defeatist mindset, and a critical spirit. Then, living a thriving life is out of the question; only survival is possible.

This perspective can be memorialized and even considered "spiritual." It's a "just enough, just in time" perspective of God. Where Scripture describes God as Jehovah Jireh (our Provider), we can depend on a constant last-minute miracle in our finances or other areas to get through life. We can begin believing this is "moral" or "honorable."

Yet, in actuality, thriving is possible. Abundance and overflow is possible.

Remember, the same power that raised Jesus from the dead lives in us. We have been given the keys to the Kingdom (Matthew 16:19). I believe that every place we set the sole of our foot, God has given us (Joshua 1:3).

Plus, we are His heirs, inheriting the Kingdom and all of the abundance that comes with it. So how do we reconcile this reality with the all too present reality that we are in a fallen world with sickness, pain, trauma, betrayal, fear, death, and disease? We embrace the truth of both.

To stick our heads in the sand and ignore the reality of the sorrow of this fallen world isn't the answer. To accept it, live

Remember, God's plan is bigger than forgiveness. It's redemption.

as a victim, admit defeat, and exist in survival mode isn't the answer either.

Though the Agape love of God ensures our eternal security (John 10:28), there is still a war that satan wages against our hearts, souls, and minds. We must remain resilient and steadfast. We must regularly feed our spirits, nourish our souls, and care for our bodies.

Mental health is, perhaps, the hot topic of our time. Anxiety, depression, addiction, and suicide are real struggles for many people. The enemy is working in countless ways to continue to deteriorate our minds.

It is up to us to renew our minds with the power of the Holy Spirit. It is up to us to take care of our souls and mental health. We can't simply sit back and expect God to do that for us. He has given us His Spirit, His truth, and free agency to do with our lives what we will.

Whatever God warns against is not because He is a killjoy but, because **He cares more than anyone else about the health of our souls.** I would argue that He even cares more than we do most of the time.

Let me give you a personal example of how I fight to care for my heart, soul, and mind, not ignoring the realities of this fallen world but not bowing to them either. Because I have a predisposition to anxiety, I must personally confront the reality of brokenness inside of me. Extended periods

He cares more than anyone else about the health of our souls.

of significant anxiety, left avoided and unaddressed, will eventually give way to depression, which I have been well acquainted with. And when I say I am predisposed to anxiety, there is science around this.

Dr. Daniel Amen is a world-renowned psychiatrist and brain disorder specialist. He shared this research in his compelling book The End of Mental Illness:

> *"In fascinating but disturbing research, fear is passed down through generations. You may be afraid of something and have absolutely no idea why. Researchers Brian Dias and Kerry Ressler from Emory University made mice afraid of a cherry blossom scent by shocking them whenever the smell was in the air. This is called classical fear conditioning in scientific circles, and this result was no surprise. What was startling, however, was that the rodents' offspring and the following generation were also afraid of the scent of cherry blossoms, even though they were never exposed to the shocks. The fear was actually transmitted epigenetically.*
>
> *The implications of this research are wide-reaching. Emotions like fear, anxiety, and perhaps even hatred may have ancestral origins. Suppose you are afraid of something and have no idea why; go back through your genealogy and look for clues that the fear may have nothing to do with your own experience.*
>
> *The stress of prior generations has also been associated*

with depression, antisocial behaviors, and memory impairment. Fortunately, it seems that stress in your ancestors can go both ways; another study suggested prior-generation stress can help animals learn to better cope with stress."

I have always felt a predisposition to anxiety and restlessness.

After many years of therapy and counseling, I couldn't uncover a particular, palpable event I thought I was searching for to explain my angst. Eventually, I became more and more curious about my genealogy. I learned that my great-grandmother had a traumatic loss of a young daughter, my grandmother's sister. My grandmother explained that my great-grandmother was never the same after that loss.

After losing her daughter, extreme caution, nervousness, worry, grief, and depression marked the rest of my great-grandmother's life, understandably. The trauma that affected my grandmother affected my mother. Now, that trauma also affects me.

I won't unpack the sins, addictions, or mental health issues in my family line. All families have their stories. All families have their tragedies. However, I am keenly aware that, at a biological level, I have some things stacked against me.

And yet, I have concluded that I am not a victim.
I am an overcomer.
I have the Spirit of God living within me.
And I choose to be whole.

Whole people are victims who choose to be responsible instead.

My parents decided to follow Jesus and break satan's legal right to our family. I am forever grateful for that. But it doesn't mean that I don't have my own fighting to do.

I take my mental, physical, emotional, and spiritual health seriously. I believe in therapy and counseling to learn how to process emotions and handle complicated feelings. I exercise regularly and am mindful of what I eat and drink. I take a tremendous amount of vitamins and supplements daily that are specifically designed to help with brain health.

I didn't always do this. The catalyst that made me start taking all of this so seriously was when I was at the lowest point of my marriage in 2016. I didn't know if my wife and I were going to make it. I had a lot of stuff in my own heart that I needed to clean up, and we were hanging on by a thread, so we started marriage counseling.

After about a year of being in sheer survival mode, eventually I hit a wall. One day I started thinking and feeling different. I was losing motivation and feeling extremely sad and defeated. Over the course of a few days it got worse and worse and I felt like I was losing my mind.

Soon things got even darker. I couldn't get out of bed. I knew that I needed help, so I went to the marriage counselor we were seeing by myself out of desperation and told him what was going on with me. He gave me some tests and diagnosed me with extreme anxiety and major depression.

For days, I remember walking around my neighborhood with such debilitating anxiety that I couldn't feel my arms. They were completely numb. Everything that I looked at had this muted gloomy filter over it. It didn't matter if it was seventy five degrees and sunny, it felt as if I was in a cave, isolated from any kind of hope or joy. Mind you, I was crushing "The American Dream," with a house, a beautiful wife, and 2 beautiful daughters. Yet I couldn't enjoy any of it. I was trying to stay alive.

As I walked, I would cry and recite Psalm 100 and Psalm 23. I remember struggling to get the words out: "The Lord is my shepherd. I shall not want..." I would beg God to help me. I would beg Him to forgive me for choices I made that I believed were causing me to feel the shame and hopelessness that I was feeling.

But all along, I was just as loved then as I am now. And God knew that the victory was mine, I just had to take it.

After a while, I decided this would not continue. I decided I was going to serve despair an eviction notice. I started an SSRI medication called Lexapro (which I was only on for a couple of weeks because I didn't like the side effects I personally experienced on it). I started eating healthier, drinking a ton of water, diffusing essential oils in the house, playing praise and worship music, speaking words of life

Whole people are victims who choose to be responsible instead.

and victory over my heart, regularly going to a therapist, and going to the gym.

One of my most vivid memories of that time was how I would get on a treadmill and run a mile or two at a very high speed, getting my heart rate up to over 160, and have a good sweat. As I ran, I would declare under my breath that I was going to be okay.

I remember dancing in the house with my family to Rend Collective's song "Counting Every Blessing" when I didn't feel like dancing.

And guess what? Slowly the darkness began to lift. I beat anxiety and depression. But it wasn't overnight.

After coming out of the darkness from this first episode of major anxiety and depression, as months and years went on, I had to figure out how to bridle anxiety and find better strategies for regulating myself instead of being overtaken by it. I still had depression come in seasons, sometimes lasting as long as two months at a time. But I believed that this would not be my permanent reality.

I hear people speak of seasonal depression as though it is an unalterable reality. I had it too, but I don't anymore. It doesn't have to be a life sentence.

The premise of Dr. Amen's book The End of Mental Illness (which I highly recommend) is that we need to stop using the language "mental health" and start framing it as "brain health" because it is our brains that affect our mentality and overall health. He says, "Get your brain healthy, and your mind will follow." I have done brain scans to see which parts of my brain need healing, and I religiously follow the health plan that Dr. Amen's team put together for me.

In addition to the health and nutrition, the supplementation, and the intentional taking care of my physical brain, I also speak the promises of God over my life. I engage in spiritual warfare by declaring Scripture aloud to combat satan's lies to steal, kill, and destroy me. Here are a few of my favorite scriptures I use for spiritual warfare:

> Death has been swallowed up in victory. "Where, O death, is your victory? Where, O death, is your sting?" The sting of death is sin, and the power of sin is the law. But thanks be to God! He gives us the victory through our Lord Jesus Christ.
>
> 1 Corinthians 15:54b-57 NIV

> "No weapon formed against you shall prosper, And every tongue which rises against you in judgment You shall condemn. This is the heritage of the servants of the Lord, And their righteousness is from Me," Says the Lord.
>
> Isaiah 54:17 NKJV

> Rejoice in the Lord always. I will say it again: Rejoice! Let your gentleness be evident to all.

The Lord is near. Do not be anxious about any-thing, but in every situation, by prayer and peti-tion, with thanksgiving, present your requests to God. And the peace of God, which transcends all understanding, will guard your hearts and your minds in Christ Jesus. Finally, brothers and sisters, whatever is true, whatever is noble, what-ever is right, whatever is pure, whatever is lovely, whatever is admirable—if anything is excellent or praiseworthy—think about such things.

Philippians 4:4-8 NIV

For we do not wrestle against flesh and blood, but against principalities, against powers, against the rulers of the darkness of this age, against spiritual hosts of wickedness in the heavenly places.

Ephesians 6:12 NKJV

For the weapons of our warfare are not carnal but mighty in God for pulling down strongholds, casting down arguments and every high thing that exalts itself against the knowledge of God, bringing every thought into captivity to the obe-dience of Christ,

II Corinthians 10:4-5 NKJV

For God has not given us a spirit of fear, but of power and of love and of a sound mind.

II Timothy 1:7 NKJV

So when Jesus had received the sour wine, He said, "It is finished!" And bowing His head, He gave up His spirit.

John 19:30 NKJV

I love to pray and talk to Jesus. I regularly enjoy communion with God through prayer, reading His Word, meditation, and singing. However, I find it interesting that the times that I feel the most tangible "state change" in my body (I'm talking about an authentic feeling in my physical body, like tingling, warmth, and adrenaline) is when I begin to speak aloud to the devil to resist him. It's when I declare these promises of God over my life, and I remind him that Jesus said, "It is finished," and the blood has canceled his legal right to me and my family.

I share all of this personal information to show you what this can look like in your life. The enemy wants to steal from you, kill you, and destroy you. You likely have a history of trauma and tragedy in your family line, but that is not a reason to act as a victim. It is merely good information to know what you are up against and better understand what satan's strategy might be against you. He's not that creative. He uses tactics and attacks through the same predispositions, addictions, and vices. And he does so generationally.

Recognize that satan (the one who hates you) wants to use everything he can to steal, kill, and destroy your joy. But He won't win. *His* fate is sealed.

But if you are in Christ, so is *yours*! Eternal life has been promised to you and is yours for the taking.

In the next chapter, we'll look at how the promise of eternal life isn't an *afterlife* thing but a *now* thing.

Eternal Life Is Now

Too many Christians think that our lives are meant to be miserably suffered through, with a "barely getting by" mentality, and then eventually, we'll die.

As you can probably tell, I was raised in a Christian home as a pastor's kid. I memorized many Bible verses, and of course, the most famous one: *"For God so loved the world, that he gave his only Son, that whoever believes in him should not perish but have eternal life."* (John 3:16 ESV).

As a kid, with your whole life ahead, you rarely think about the possibility of your own death. These verses, while powerful, felt distant to me. Like most people, I assumed they only refer to living in Heaven or this strange idea of "the afterlife."

But as time has gone on, the Holy Spirit has revealed some things that have dramatically shifted my perspective. I'm not talking about simply getting older and maturing. Many people get older without growing in maturity at all. But that's beside the point. I'm talking about revelation from the Spirit of God to affect how I live, love, and lead *today*. As in right now.

As a pastor, when I read the New Testament, I pay close attention to Paul's words to Timothy. Paul was an apostolic leader who mentored Timothy, a young pastor. He gives Timothy many insights that have been incredibly applicable to me regarding how I lead.

There was one particular charge that he gave Timothy that has jumped out to me and, in many ways, was the inspiration for writing this book:

Fight the good fight of the faith. **Take hold** of the eternal life to which you were called.

1 Timothy 6:12 NIV

This consideration went against my elementary under-standing of eternal life as being confined to the afterlife. Paul wasn't writing this to a dead person when he wrote this. He was writing it to a living person! And if eternal life was something that a living person could experience, I was curious about exactly what that looked like.

Before getting further into that, a few other scripture refer-ences helped reveal to me that one thing was sure: **the full-ness of life God has for His people isn't something we receive by accident or haphazardly. It's something that we seize, that we take hold of.**

Consider these verses.

Paul also said:

> "Not that I have already obtained all this, or have already arrived at my goal, but I press on to **take hold** of that for which Christ Jesus **took hold** of me."

Philippians 3:12 NIV

Jesus said:

> "And from the days of John the Baptist until now the kingdom of heaven suffers violence, and the violent **take it by force.**"

Matthew 11:12 NKJV

The fullness of life God has for His people isn't something we receive by accident or haphazardly. It's something that we seize, that we take hold of.

When Jesus said these words, He wasn't saying that the Kingdom of Heaven was suffering violence negatively or as if it could be in danger somehow. He said that people were so hungry for the truth, reconciliation, the Kingdom of God, and the fullness of life that they were passionate about acquiring it. People mobbed Jesus wherever He went.

A group of men even cut a hole in the roof of a building to lower a paralyzed man down into Jesus so He could heal him. (Mark 2:2-11) This action was them truly taking the initiative and actively pursuing something they wanted, not simply hoping it came to them.

This eternal life is more than forgiveness of sin and salvation. Salvation is a gift God gives those who repent of their sin and admit their need for His redemption. You cannot work for it, and it's undeserved. *"It is by grace that we are saved"* (Ephesians 2:8-9).

Timothy was already saved when Paul wrote to him to "take hold of the eternal life to which he had been called." Paul was already saved when he wrote Philippians 3. Note the distinction between the promise of salvation (the forgiveness of sin with the promise of Heaven after death) and the taking hold of eternal life *today*.

Taking hold of eternal life is taking hold of the Kingdom. *Now.*

You can be saved and still not understand the principles of being an heir of the Kingdom of God.

Jesus said:

> "I will give you the **keys of the kingdom of heaven,** and whatever you bind on earth shall be bound in heaven, and whatever you loose on earth shall be loosed in heaven."
>
> Matthew 16:19 ESV

A pastor friend once told me he was frustrated about having limited access to the massive church his dad had founded. Being a pastor's kid who is called to ministry can be complicated and frustrating. In this case, his dad had given him a key that he thought was just to the offices, so he often had to call a maintenance worker to open up the auditorium when he wanted to go in and play the piano and worship. His father was in charge of the church, yet he still was forced regularly to ask for special access to everything his father owned.

That's what it can be like for you and me. We can be saved but still view ourselves as peasants, essentially wandering the streets of this great Kingdom like we're undercover, scared that we will be discovered as frauds who have no business being there.

My pastor friend was frustrated because he would have to wait for a maintenance person to grant him daily access to the 5,000-seat sanctuary. Every day, he waited, sometimes

30 minutes at a time, and every day, his frustration grew. "Why do I always have to wait for someone else?" he thought to himself. After many years and the tragic passing of his father, he discovered something surprising.

One day, while waiting again to receive access, he had another moment of frustration. For some reason, he decided to try his key to confirm it would not open the sanctuary door. To his shock, the key actually worked! That's when he discovered that he had spent years waiting to receive something that he already had but never used. What he had worked the whole time. He was asking for access, but his father already gave him the master key to the entire facility...a long time ago.

We fail to realize that because of the blood of Jesus, we don't have to wander the streets and beg for food. We are heirs of the Kingdom and co-heirs with Christ (Romans 8:17). God does not simply tolerate us, but we have total access to His entire Kingdom!

If we have keys, we have access.

If we have access, we have the right to the riches of the Kingdom that God has given us access to possess.

Don't let anyone tell you anything different.

Too many Christians think that our lives are meant to be miserably suffered through, with a "barely getting by" mentality, and then eventually, we'll die. *Then, finally,* we'll get to experience the goodness and the treasure of the Kingdom of God. No wonder many Christians are crabby, critical, and hostile; their theology stinks!

If you have access to the Kingdom, then it is helpful to understand what this Kingdom is all about. The Kingdom of God is about healing and wholeness. It's about reconciliation and forgiveness. It's about love, holiness, prosperity, and purpose.

This is the eternal life that God has called us to receive. It is both in the afterlife and the now-life. When Jesus came to earth, He showed us what the Kingdom was about. He healed miraculously, forgave sin, and brought dead people back to life. He also confronted empty religion and oppression.

You don't have to just "get by." You don't have to have a "just enough, just in time" theology of God. God is your Father. He is Jehovah Jireh - your provider. He is the One who "owns the cattle on a thousand hills" (Psalm 50:10). He is the One who created the earth and everything in it, the world and all who live in it (Psalm 24:1). So why would we expect just enough to survive barely? Don't you know that Your Father wants you to thrive?

Let's clearly define what we're talking about here. I'm not merely talking about having a lot of money. The Bible is clear that the love of money is the root of all evil (1 Timothy

Taking hold of eternal life is taking hold of the Kingdom. *Now.*

6:10). What I am saying, however, is that if you have always limited God and limited what you believe is possible regarding His provision for your life, you might not understand the access you have been given.

It might be possible that you don't realize how big your God is.

It might be possible that you don't understand who you are.

God created you with the capacity for breakthrough, building generous wealth, and bringing God's love and healing to the world in a way you could have never imagined.

If eternal life is *now*, and if you've been given keys to the Kingdom yet lived well beneath what is possible, let me ask you a question: Why? Who is holding you back?

The answer isn't someone else. It's not "the system." It's not your mother or father. It's certainly not God. It's not even satan, though he'd love for you to continue living well beneath what is possible.

Have you considered that the problem might be you?

That can be hard to swallow, but it is good news. It's good news because it means you don't have to wait for anyone else to escape the scarcity mindset and the "barely getting by" mentality.

You can choose to step out of it *yourself.*

Once again, if *you're* the dwelling place of God, if *you've* been called to eternal life now, and if *you've* been given the keys to the Kingdom, then you have access. The only thing left to do is give yourself permission to receive it...

Giving Yourself Permission

"God has the most *accurate* view of you, but you have the most *powerful* view of you."

I'll never forget when my friend and high performance coach Christian Santiago asked me this question. "Who has the most powerful view of you?" I gave him an elementary Christian answer, "Umm, God, I guess." It seemed appropriate to say that God has the most robust view of me. I mean, God is the Creator. He's the author of all living things. He formed and fashioned me.

Christian said, "No. God has the most *accurate* view of you, but you have the most *powerful* view of you."

Christian was trying to show me that my thoughts, feelings, emotions, and actions would follow my self-perception. Even though God has the most accurate view of us, if we have an inaccurate idea of ourselves, those limiting beliefs will direct our thoughts, feelings, emotions, and actions.

These limiting beliefs come primarily from our upbringing, our inward thoughts, and our closest inner circle of people. My mom and dad are the most extraordinary people on the planet. They love God, and they love people with their whole hearts. They have worked incredibly hard to obey God by starting an incredible church and sacrificing more than anyone I know to set their children up for success.

For nine years, my dad would drive us to and from school every day, from West Boca Raton to East Fort Lauderdale, about an hour there and an hour back. It was worth it for him because the private Christian school in Fort Lauderdale was the only one willing to give our family a significant deduction in tuition by considering our family's income and pioneering church work. The idea of "where there's a will, there's a way" was a hallmark of how my parents raised me and my sister; we are both grateful for that.

But some things informed my parents' view of themselves, which inevitably kept them from doing even more. For quite some time, this also set a limiting precedent for what I believed was possible.

When my dad was nine, his father left him and his family. They were already poor, but his mom then had to work multiple jobs around the clock to try and provide for him and his three siblings. My dad vividly remembers his mom giving him and his siblings a quarter to walk down to a McDonald's. They would use the money to buy a single hamburger and split it four ways so they would have something to eat.

When my dad was much older, he began to serve in ministry. Some of the things they learned in their early years of serving in churches made them extra cautious when it came to church finances. When he felt the call of God to start his church, he was committed to ensuring it operated with the utmost financial integrity.

This is a notion that many would regard as honorable, and it most definitely is. But in hindsight, my dad will admit that there is some nuance to the proper application of this principle. His meager upbringing and his experiences in local ministry caused him to do an "over-correction" when pastoring his church and leading our family. He always felt very uncomfortable talking about finances in church, and in our family, we lived by a "just enough" mentality.

I'm aware that this can mean different things to different people. Applying a "just enough" mentality told us that we always believed God for just enough to pay our bills, to eat, and to tithe.

As a result, family vacations, adventures, eating out, the joy of blessing others, and giving offerings above our tithe were scarce opportunities. It was the quintessential "scarcity mindset" that is unfortunately spiritualized in many Christian circles.

As a dramatic counter to the unhealthy "prosperity gospel," Christians can also develop a "poverty gospel."

The poverty gospel is when it is seen as righteous and noble to barely get by and always be forced to pray for a miraculous gift just to survive. I'm not saying our family embraced the poverty gospel entirely, but we lived by at least some form of it. If I'm being honest, it never sat right with me.

I think differently now. I now believe that the "just enough" mentality is a selfish way of thinking. If you think about it, having just enough to survive yourself means that you aren't able to do what Jesus said in Matthew 6, which is to give to people in need. How can you provide if there's only enough for you to survive?

As a dramatic counter to the unhealthy "prosperity gospel," Christians can also develop a "poverty gospel."

If you only have just enough, you can't obey what Proverbs 22 says, "The generous will themselves be blessed, for they share their food with the poor."

There are numerous other scriptures that you simply cannot abide by if there is no overflow.

I'll never forget what the legendary Pastor Larry Stockstill told me one day. He leaned over and said in his endearing Louisiana accent, "If it ain't in the well, it ain't coming up in the bucket." His point was that we cannot give others what we do not possess.

This is true in many areas, of course. For example, we can't give the Father's love if we haven't received it. If we haven't received forgiveness for ourselves, we can't offer it to others. And in the same way, if we are financially needy, there is no overflow for us to bless others financially in their times of need. So the "just enough" mentality is very selfish, and based on the few scripture references noted here, it's unbiblical.

Someone might say, "But wait, doesn't Jesus say in Matthew 6 to seek first the Kingdom of God, and all these things will be added unto you?" Of course, He does, and intimacy with God should always be our top priority.

But it doesn't say it's the only thing that we seek. It simply says, *"Seek first."*

It doesn't say we should avoid hard work, dreaming big, or believing in God for more. On the contrary, Scripture tells us that God can do "exceedingly and abundantly above what we could ask or imagine" (Ephesians 3:20).

As we seek God first, out of the overflow of intimacy with Him, we go out, work hard, and believe God for abundance. "All these things" are not added to us by sitting, praying, and expecting our bank accounts to have zeros added to them.

These things come from hard work, too. But it's more than just about working hard. It's also about working smart. It's about doing things with excellence.

I heard a pastor once say regarding the financial provision, "Some of you are praying for miracles when you ought to be working on mastery." He's right. Because money follows mastery. Proverbs 22:29 says, *"Do you see someone skilled in their work? They will serve before kings; they will not serve before officials of low rank."*

We understand this concept on a fundamental level. You've likely heard the saying, "You get what you pay for." If you needed a life-saving surgery, would you want a discount surgeon or a surgeon ranked in the top 1%? You would want the top 1% surgeon with an incredible track record, and I'm positive you'd be willing to pay more for it!

Money follows mastery, and excellence matters.

You can make excuses, or you can make progress. But you can't make both.

There could be many different categories that you need to give yourself permission in. For me, it was money. For you, it could be permitting yourself to be a better mother or father than the one you had growing up. It could be starting a business or a ministry that can bless others. It could be the goal of improving your mental health or breaking addiction's chains. It could be to take dominion over your physical fitness or your diet. It could be to put your form of art out into the world. Whatever it is, you should do it with an abundance mindset, with a spirit of excellence, as though you're working for God (Colossians 3:23-24).

Daniel distinguished himself from everyone else in the kingdom of Babylon with his excellence, so the king appointed him over the whole kingdom.

King David was such an excellent musician that it brought him before the king of Israel.

Joshua and Caleb had "different spirits" about them because they believed God could give them victory over giants in the Promised Land that no one else thought they could defeat. *That* is an excellent mindset.

You can make excuses, or you can make progress. But you can't make both.

Too many people are content just to "play it safe." We should remember Jesus' parable of the talents in Matthew

25. Because it has informed my abundance mindset, I will include the entire Biblical text in this chapter:

> For it will be like a man going on a journey, who called his servants and entrusted to them his property. To one he gave five talents, to another two, to another one, to each according to his ability. Then he went away. He who had received the five talents went at once and traded with them, and he made five talents more. So also he who had the two talents made two talents more. But he who had received the one talent went and dug in the ground and hid his master's money. Now after a long time the master of those servants came and settled accounts with them. And he who had received the five talents came forward, bringing five talents more, saying, 'Master, you delivered to me five talents; here, I have made five talents more.' His master said to him, 'Well done, good and faithful servant. You have been faithful over a little; I will set you over much. Enter into the joy of your master.' And he also who had the two talents came forward, saying, 'Master, you delivered to me two talents; here, I have made two talents more.' His master said to him, 'Well done, good and faithful servant. You have been faithful over a little; I will set you over much. Enter into the joy of your master.' He also who had received the one talent came forward, saying, 'Master, I knew you to be a hard man, reaping where you

did not sow, and gathering where you scattered no seed, so I was afraid, and I went and hid your talent in the ground. Here, you have what is yours.' But his master answered him, 'You wicked and slothful servant! You knew that I reap where I have not sown and gather where I scattered no seed? Then you ought to have invested my money with the bankers, and at my coming I should have received what was my own with interest. So take the talent from him and give it to him who has the ten talents. For to everyone who has will more be given, and he will have an abundance. But from the one who has not, even what he has will be taken away. And cast the worthless servant into the outer darkness. In that place there will be weeping and gnashing of teeth.'

Matthew 25:14-30 ESV

What a severe response the master gave to the servant who buried the one talent! I could easily argue the case of that servant. Number one, it wasn't his money. The thought of doing something with someone else's money was scary to him. Number two, what if things didn't work out? And three, what if he ended up with less than he was initially given? To that, the master said he should have at least put it in the bank for that measly .0001% interest rate. But the other two servants doubled the money that was given to them, which the master praised.

Did you catch part of the masters' response? He took that small amount that he entrusted to the "slothful servant" and gave it to the one who already had an abundance! Why? Because of his mindset.

The servant given five talents, and the servant given two talents gave themselves *permission* to double what was given them. They didn't take the opportunity for granted.

You should not take for granted that God has given you talents and purpose. You should take what He's given you and run with it! This is "the taking!" This is part of what taking hold of eternal life looks like!

I believe this message is for someone who is reading this right now. I believe this is a holy moment and can change your life trajectory.

You hold the keys.
Stop thinking too small!

You've developed a view of your God that is too small!

Though He owns "the cattle on a thousand hills" (Psalm 50:10), "you *have* not because you *ask* not" (James 4:2).

You've also had too small a view of yourself, and you have yet to see yourself as the ruler, ambassador, and co-heir with Christ that you are. It's time for that to change.

You should not take for granted that God has given you talents and purpose. You should take what He's given you and run with it!

Get alone with God right now. Permit yourself to a new reality that glorifies Christ, takes hold of the Kingdom's abundance, and seizes the eternal life to which you've been called. Renounce any curses spoken over you that have held you down, made you afraid, or kept you thinking small.

God doesn't want you to have "just enough" to get by. Whether it's talent, faith, finances, love, etc., "just enough" falls short of what the Creator of the universe wants for you.

Consider the two servants who multiplied what was given to them. Now, go and do likewise.

Humble, Holy Swagger

I've never met a Christian who accomplished greatness without also having a humble and holy swagger.

The best news in the world is that you are not alone.

You don't have to fight this battle alone.

More than a significant other, a family member, or an excellent friend, you have someone much closer to you than any other could ever be. I'm talking about The Helper—the Holy Spirit.

Jesus said:

> "Nevertheless I tell you the truth. It is to your advantage that I go away; for if I do not go away, the Helper will not come to you; but if I depart, I will send Him to you."
>
> John 16:7 NKJV

He was speaking to His disciples when He said this. But how could Him leaving them be an "advantage"? He was the Messiah, the Promised One, the Son of God standing right there in their midst. He cast out demons in front of their very eyes. He healed the sick. He brought people that were dead back to life.

If I were one of the disciples, I would have wanted to cling to Him for dear life and not let Him go anywhere.

But it was to their advantage because Jesus, who was God, one with His Father, came in the flesh. But the Holy Spirit wouldn't come in the flesh but would rest on and dwell within every believer. When Jesus could only be in one place at a time, the Holy Spirit could be in all areas simultaneously.

While Jesus was there to show the way and inspire, the Holy Spirit empowered them to do what He did. This is how it could be to their advantage that He would go away.

And it's the best news in the world that we don't have faith in a God who did something incredible thousands of years ago, but we have faith that *that* same God lives in us today and empowers us to do the supernatural.

This is Christianity as it *could* be.

The "taking hold of eternal life" isn't something we are left to try and figure out on our own. We are supernaturally empowered to do it by the Spirit of God that lives within us.

I don't know about you, but I can get discouraged trying to live a supernatural life in my strength. If I do it in my power, I can get exhausted trying to "take hold" of this eternal life. The most disheartening thing is the struggle to resist sin by sheer willpower or heaping guilt or shame on myself.

That's because it's not supposed to be this way.

Romans 8:26 has become one of my favorite scriptures. It says, "Likewise the Spirit also helps in our weaknesses." (Romans 8:26a) In this reference, the Greek word for

It's the best news in the world that we don't have faith in a God who did something incredible thousands of years ago, but we have faith that *that* same God lives in us today and empowers us to do the supernatural.

"helps" is ***sunantilambanomai***, which literally means (get ready for this), "to take hold together against."

When I learned that the meaning of this word specifically used the words "take hold," it melted my brain. We and the Holy Spirit take hold together against whatever the trouble is. Whatever problems we are facing, we are not alone.

King David wasn't alone when He faced Goliath.

Shadrach, Meschach, and Abednego were not alone when they were thrown into a fiery furnace.

Harriet Tubman wasn't alone when she escaped slavery and helped free approximately 70 enslaved people via The Underground Railroad.

C.S. Lewis wasn't alone when he wrote his captivating books, which have been translated into over thirty languages and sold millions of copies worldwide.

The single mother isn't alone in trying to provide for her family and show up emotionally.

The husband, who is losing hope that his marriage will ever see daybreak, isn't alone.

The business owner feeling financial pressure, staff layoffs, and battling crippling anxiety isn't alone.

The Pastor trying to bring people to Jesus, facing endless criticism and feeling like nothing will ever be good enough, isn't alone.

But in all these circumstances, each person must fully show up. You and I are required to show up. The good news is that the Holy Spirit will show up, too. And that is our supernatural advantage.

When you fully show up and are submitted to God, drawing on the power of the Holy Spirit who lives in you, He brings the "super" to your "natural."

So the next time you wonder if you can do this and have what it takes, remember your advantage. Whether you're considering taking a risk to start a new business or trying to resist the urge to look at porn, go deep to where the Spirit of God dwells inside of you. Take a breath and draw on the power of God.

The God of the open ocean, the One who created wildlife, the artisan who dreamt up music, landscapes, sunsets, love, sex, and laughter dwells in you and doesn't want you ever to feel alone. He doesn't want you ever frivolously to strive for your strength; He knows how exhausting and depressing that can be.

The Holy Spirit knows everything about you and the one who hates you. He knows what satan's plans are for you. He knows they are to steal, kill, and destroy. But He is determined to give you life and give it to you abundantly.

Revelation 12:11 says that we overcome satan "by the blood of the lamb and the word of our testimony."

Jesus' blood shed on the cross has canceled the curse of sin over us, and when we outwardly speak the testimony of what He has done for us, the Holy Spirit activates within us and "takes hold together against" satan and his fallen angels.

Sometimes, we have to actually speak out loud directly against the enemy's attacks against us. "The blood of the lamb" was Jesus' part. "The word of our testimony" is our part.

In the 4th Century, a Christian monk named Evagrius made this understandable through the concept of "Monastic Antirrhesis," which means to "refute and contradict." This principle involves talking back to the enemy and demonic forces using Scripture to defeat their oppressive attacks. (Go back to Chapter 3 for some practical examples of this.)

Evagrius says, "Our Lord Jesus Christ, who handed on to us everything [necessary] for salvation, bestowed on us [power] 'to trample serpents and scorpions, and all the powers of evil.'...handed on to us what He Himself did when tempted by satan. And so in the moment of battle, when the demons attack and hurl weapons against us, we too [like Christ], must speak out against them from the

No curse, no lie, no fear, no depression, no anxiety, no sickness, disease, or even death stands a chance against God and doesn't stand a chance against us, the dwelling place of God.

[text of] sacred Scripture. In this way the[ir] foul thoughts will not persist in us."

This monk understood what many of us have forgotten: **No curse, no lie, no fear, no depression, no anxiety, no sickness, disease, or even death stands a chance against God and doesn't stand a chance against us, the dwelling place of God.** Because even in death, the enemy doesn't win. We will live forever in union with The Living God. It is good for us to remember:

> For He Himself has said, "I will never leave you nor forsake you." So we may **boldly** say: "The Lord is my helper; I will not fear. What can man do to me?
>
> Hebrews 13:5a-6 NKJV

We have the Holy Spirit, the supernatural advantage. Embracing this brings boldness that is otherworldly.

I've never met a Christian who accomplished greatness without also having a humble and holy swagger.

We should walk with this swagger, knowing that each step is in step with The Divine.

We face fear. We give thanks. We take risks. We sing praise. We regularly remind ourselves of the truth. We remember Who He is and who we are. With the help of The Helper, we take ground and rebuild ruins.

Rebuilding Ruins

It's scandalous.
It doesn't
make sense.
It's shocking, and
it's beautiful.

There are different types of rulers.

There are good ones, and there are evil ones.

Oppressive ones and protective ones.

Narcissistic ones and benevolent ones.

God is a benevolent ruler. When He created man, He immediately created him with power and authority. From the very beginning of time, God graciously shared His rulership. He didn't dominate or control, though He easily could have.

God didn't create man because He was bored, sad, or lonely. God The Trinity (Father, Son, and Holy Spirit) was in perfect loving union with Himself.

Out of the overflow of perfect love from this union, He created man to lavish His love on Him and share the beauty of His loving kindness. As previously covered in this book, tragically, sin entered the world when man rebelled against God. That's when the perfect living conditions were compromised.

When sin entered the world, so did death, decay, fear, and everything that separates man from God and crushes his spirit.

God hates this.

God doesn't only hate sin because He is holy. He hates it because He hates the trauma it causes His beloved children.

And God has made His rescue mission clear. He sent His Son Jesus into the world to save the world.

Jesus is King.

There has never been anyone like Him to walk the face of the earth. He did incredible things, and He is still doing extraordinary things.

Just before Jesus definitively started His ministry, right after His face-off with satan that the 2nd chapter of this book talked about, He made a bold public announcement. He stood up in the synagogue and read from the scroll of Isaiah. He said,

> "The Spirit of the Lord is on me, because he has anointed me to proclaim good news to the poor. He has sent me to proclaim freedom for the prisoners and recovery of sight for the blind, to set the oppressed free, to proclaim the year of the Lord's favor."
>
> Luke 4:18-19 NIV

He then went on to say,

> "Today, this scripture is fulfilled in your hearing."
>
> Luke 4:21b NIV

God doesn't only hate sin because He is holy. He hates it because He hates the trauma it causes His beloved children.

This declaration was staggering because He was announcing that He was the Son of God and came to do His Father's will to defeat satan and reconcile a lost and hurting world. That's why we worship Jesus! That's why we thank Him!

That's why we celebrate the story of Christmas and Easter and anxiously await the renewal of all things at the end of time. It's truly a beautiful story.

But we have to know our place in the story. Because it's not just Jesus that does the Father's will; we do, too. It's not just Jesus who came here with a purpose; He also calls us to rebuild ruins.

Let's take a closer look at the words of the prophecy through Isaiah that Jesus was quoting:

> "The Spirit of the Lord God is upon Me, Because the Lord has anointed Me To preach good tidings to the poor; He has sent Me to heal the brokenhearted, To proclaim liberty to the captives, And the opening of the prison to those who are bound; To proclaim the acceptable year of the Lord, And the day of vengeance of our God; To comfort all who mourn, To console those who mourn in Zion, To give them beauty for ashes, The oil of joy for mourning, The garment of praise for the spirit of heaviness; That they may be called trees of righteousness, The planting of the Lord, that He may be glorified." And they shall rebuild the

old ruins, They shall raise up the former desolations, And they shall repair the ruined cities, The desolations of many generations."

Isaiah 61:1-4 NKJV

Did you see it? It can be easy to miss. After it talks about all of the beautiful things that Jesus came to do, it seamlessly flows into prophesying about what we will do!

Look at it again with emphasis added:

> "And **they** shall rebuild the old ruins, **They** shall raise up the former desolations, And **they** shall repair the ruined cities, The desolations of many generations."
>
> Isaiah 61:4 NKJV

Jesus came to earth to rebuild the ruins, but He never intended to do it alone.

He invites us into the fight. He has breathed the Holy Spirit into us, and we have His power!

> But if the Spirit of Him who raised Jesus from the dead dwells in you, He who raised Christ from the dead will also give life to your mortal bodies through His Spirit who dwells in you.
>
> Romans 8:11 NKJV

Jesus is our elder brother (Hebrews 2:11), and we are joining in His fight in this fallen world to rebuild the ruins for His

Jesus came to earth to rebuild the ruins, but He never intended to do it alone.

glory and the good of all. Jesus has given us the same glory God gave Him (John 17:22), so now we do what He does.

We are lovers. We are reconcilers. We are benevolent rulers.

God's power and authority given to us has never been for pride or selfish gain; it's been to do what God does: redeem, restore, and rebuild.

As God's heart breaks for people who are disillusioned, depressed, addicted, and hopeless, so does ours.

As God's Word breathes life into their broken spirits, so do we!

We speak life. We pick up. We lift burdens.

We remind people who they are!

With momentous intentionality and exceptional attention to detail, we have been formed and fashioned, placed on the earth at this specific time, for this purpose. With the Holy Spirit living inside us, we do what God and Jesus do! We've been invited into this glory!

It's scandalous. It doesn't make sense. It's shocking, and it's beautiful.

It reminds me of the story of the prophet Ezekiel and the dry bones in Ezekiel 37. In this story, the prophet has a

God's power and authority given to us has never been for pride or selfish gain; it's been to do what God does: redeem, restore, and rebuild.

supernatural vision of standing in a place with a collection of dry bones. God tells the prophet that those bones represent His chosen people, Israel. Then He asks Ezekiel, "Can these bones live?"

I'm sure the prophet was confused by this question and its implications. "You alone know", he replied. Rather than explaining, God tells *him* to prophesy to those bones. Supernaturally, they began to come together and form bodies. What was dry and lifeless before became living flesh.

This is the same symbolic power that we have today! It's never just another day at the office. Every day is an opportunity to rebuild ruins where the enemy has broken in and broken down.

But just as valid as it is that it's never just another day at the office, I can guarantee that there are ruins that need to be restored in your office: people's marriages, dreams, and destinies.

Consider your own before you worry about other people's ruins.

What has the enemy stolen from you?

What lies has he told you that you've agreed with?

What people, places, or things have you given up on that you wish you hadn't?

With the authority of Christ, take back what the enemy has stolen. Don't walk in fear. Curse the things that have tried to curse you. Rebuild those ruins.

Satan hates to be reminded that you have been made alive together with Christ and raised with Him, made to sit with Him in the heavenly places (Ephesians 2:4-6).

Knowing and exercising your authority over satan and your ruins, now go help others! Rebuild, renew, and restore! Prophesy words of life, awakening, and breakthrough over people and places that need it.

Go to places others are too afraid to go and know that the power of God is with you.

No one cares more about the ruins than God does. So don't hesitate. Go in His strength!

Too many are just trying to survive, but they've been placed here at this specific time for a particular purpose, just like you have. They are orphans, widows, neighbors, friends, lovers, and strangers. But more than that, they are children of God, created in God's image and rulers. They may not know it yet.

This is why Jesus taught us to pray, "Thy Kingdom come, Thy will be done on earth as it is in heaven." Ruins matter; they burden the heart of God, but you are a part of His plan to reconcile what has been lost.

What has the enemy stolen from you?

What lies has he told you that you've agreed with?

What people, places, or things have you given up on that you wish you hadn't?

Friend, it's your time.

You're here right now, and it's not an accident.

It's time to think bigger, to realize you're even more than forgiven; you're empowered.

It's time to receive the abundance mindset, reject the survival mentality, embrace your benevolent rulership, and rebuild the ruins.

So, look at the dry bones around you. Do you believe they can live? Hear the word of the Lord! Speak to them! Prophesy!

Fight the good fight of faith and **take hold** of the eternal life that you've been called to.

Because good things come to those who take.

The Sound Mind

A 30 DAY JOURNEY TO CONQUERING FEAR
AND TAKING HOLD OF YOUR FUTURE

This is a 7 day excerpt of
"The Sound Mind" devotional.

The full version is 30 days and includes
daily reflection questions.

Coming 2024

Contents

Neuroplasticity & Mastering Your Mind

But this I call to mind, and therefore I have hope: The steadfast love of the Lord never ceases; his mercies never come to an end; they are new every morning; great is your faithfulness. "The Lord is my portion," says my soul, "therefore I will hope in him."

Lamentations 3:21-24 ESV

Message

Neuroplasticity is the ability of the brain to form and reorganize synaptic connections, especially in response to learning or experience or following injury.

Our brains are always changing. Through our thought patterns we create neural pathways, which over time create mindsets and default ways of how we perceive life, relationships, adversity, etc.

Every night as we sleep, new baby nerve cells are born into our brains. This is called neurogenesis. And every morning when we wake up, it is up to us as to what we are going to do with those new baby nerve cells. We are either going to use them wisely, removing bad thoughts and conquering bad habits, or we are going to use them against ourselves and solidify negative thinking patterns and toxic habits.

God isn't only a God of second chances. He's the God who gives us new mercies every single day. And the scripture in Lamentations about His love and mercy being new every morning and never coming to an end, is only substantiated in science when we consider neuroplasticity and new baby nerve cells born into our brains every night as we sleep!

Child of God, you have been given power. 2 Timothy 1:7 says, "For God has not given us a spirit of fear, but of power and of love and of a sound mind." (NKJV). And the English Standard Version says, "power, love, and *self-control.*" The New Living Translation says, "power, love, and *self-discipline.*"

Remember that you are not in a "fixed state." The brain is always changing. Thought patterns can change. New ones can be formed. The brain is neuroplastic, ever changing. Take your God-given authority over your mind because you have a sound mind, self-control, and self-discipline. Yes you do! Take good care of those new baby nerve cells born into your brains and thank God for His new mercies every morning. How will you act? What thoughts will you allow to ruminate? What patterns or habits will you choose today? They will either serve you or war against your peace.

You are not alone! It's the best news ever that God's love and faithfulness never ends! Take heart and hope in Him.

Prayer

Thank You God that I have a sound mind. Thank You God that You have given me power over my brain, my mind, over my past, and grace to direct my future. I can't control circumstances, but I can hope in You and I can have a sound mind no matter what I am facing. I rely on our one-ness today, God. I need You today and every day. I can't do this on my own.

Please bless my mental health, as I will participate with You in the renewing of my mind with the power of the Holy Spirit. I'm not going back. I'm moving ahead. I declare right now in the Name of Jesus that my past is over. I am new! You make all things new!

Amen!

Grab Fear By The Tail

Then the Lord said to Moses, "Reach out your hand and take it by the tail" (and he reached out his hand and caught it, and it became a rod in his hand),

Exodus 4:4 NKJV

Message

When God appeared to Moses and told Him he was going to use him to deliver His people, Moses was afraid. He doubted. He debated. "So the Lord said to him, "What is that in your hand?" He said, "A rod." And He said, "Cast it on the ground." So he cast it on the ground, and it became a serpent; and Moses fled from it." Exodus 4:2 -3 NKJV

If Moses was afraid before at the very *idea* of facing *Pharoah*, He became even more fearful when his staff turned into a serpent. Any wildlife expert will tell you that you should not pick up a snake by its tail because it elicits a panic response in the snake, and it can easily turn and bite you. God of course knew this, but He still told Moses to "take it by the tail." When Moses obeyed God and picked it up by the tail, it miraculously turned back into a staff in his hand.

Just as the staff was a tool in the hand of Moses, so was Pharaoh a tool in the hand of God. "For the Scripture says to Pharaoh, 'For this very purpose I have raised you up, that I might show my power in you, and that my name might be proclaimed in all the earth." Romans 9:17 ESV

God knew that Pharaoh would snarl, hiss, and snap back at Moses, just as a snake would, being picked up by its tail. But God calls us to do dangerous things in order for His power to be displayed, and our faith to be built. We can become less and less afraid the more and more we put ourselves in positions to see the manifestation of God's power in our unsettling circumstances.

Don't run from fear like Moses originally did. Run straight at it and grab it by its tail. We can actually take heart knowing that even if things do seem to go sideways, we are protected and covered no matter what. "If the snake bites you," (so to speak), know that you will not die. You actually have Almighty God, Jehovah Shammah, living in you that will protect you from the enemy's type of venom. Just like when Paul was bitten by a venomous serpent, he "shook off the creature in the fire and suffered no harm." (Acts 28:5 ESV).

Prayer

God, give me the kind of confidence that can run straight at fear, not away from it. You have given me a spirit of power, love, and a sound mind, not a spirit of fear. I know that my only way to grow is to face fear. I know that nothing miraculous happens in my comfort zone. I want my faith and confidence in You to increase, so help me face the unsettling circumstances, have the courageous conversations, make the hard decisions, and go to the scary places. Go with me. Lead me. I love You, God.

Amen.

It Gets Better

Weeping may last through the night, but joy comes with the morning.

Psalm 30:5b NLT

Message

Many people deal with mental and emotional pain. I know that I have. Mental health is a major topic of conversation and concern for people today. I recently went to California and as we headed east just outside of San Diego we began to drive through mountains with massive boulders all over them. The first sight of the boulders immediately brought me back to a place of remembrance of a difficult time.

The last time that I had been driving through similar boulders in California was more than 4 years prior. At that time, I was dealing with significant anxiety and depression. In fact, around that time I would often have to "bow out" from preaching opportunities because of how much pressure and anxiety I would feel leading up to the messages. Thankfully, my dad was always there to step in and preach for me.

When I was in California 4 years prior, I was there with a creative team to shoot videos that I had worked really hard on for months by dreaming them up, scripting and story-boarding them, and was to be one of the people in front of the camera communicating the main message. The only problem was the week leading up to the trip, the anxiety was so significant that I was desperately searching for a way out. I was adamantly thinking about if there was anyone else that could do my portions of the video. There wasn't anyone else. I dug deep and by the grace of God flew out to California and did the videos.

I'm so glad that I did. There wasn't anyone else that could do them the way that I did. And I don't say that arrogantly, I say it because God put that vision in *my* heart. Not someone else's. And it came pouring out of me.

This time around in California, seeing the boulders again, they took me back. They took me back to see God's faithfulness and my healing journey. They reminded me that there were times when it consistently felt like the world was caving in around me and I would have to bow out because I couldn't take the pressure. I remember worrying that would be how the rest of my life would be, or an even scarier thought that somehow it could get worse. I remember never being able to see a light at the end of the tunnel. But I don't feel that way now. The sight of these boulders made me recognize how far I'd come.

Our God is Jehovah Jireh, which means He is our doctor. He is our healer. He is the healer of our bodies, spirits, *and* our minds. His mercies are new every morning. We have to put one foot in front of the other. Do the necessary work to work through trauma, disappointment, addiction, and emotional turmoil. I had to keep moving and believing God for my healing, while actively engaging in prayer, confession, safe friendships, therapy, and evaluating my physical health. I'm by no means perfect, and I still have difficult days, but they don't last as long, and they are fewer and farther between.

Do not believe the lie that there is no hope. Hear this from me personally: **it gets better.** It doesn't necessarily get easier, but you get stronger. Take it one day at a time, friend. You will soon have your own boulders in your life that serve as reminders that God never left you, that His mercies have sustained you, and that you are doing better than you thought possible. It's time to align your thinking with the hope and healing of the Kingdom of God.

Prayer

God of my mind, body, and spirit. I need You. I need Your hope. I pray that You would move in power in me and that You would help me renew my mind. I believe You for breakthrough in my mental health and that sorrow is only for a season, but joy is coming. Heal my mind and body as I sleep. Heal my heart as I give You my trust. I *choose* to believe that it gets better! I choose joy! Thank you for healing, Jesus!

Amen.

Towdah (Expectant Praise)

In God I have put my trust; I will not be afraid. What can man do to me? Vows made to You are binding upon me, O God; I will render praises (towdah) to You.

Psalm 56:11-12 NKJV

Message

There are seven different Hebrew words for "praise" found in the Old Testament:

Yadah, Halal, Zamar, Towdah, Tehillah, Shabach, and Barak. Most English Bible translations have just translated all of these variations into one simple word "praise." The issue here is that the seven variations lose their individual meanings by distilling them so succinctly. It's like how in the New Testament there are 4 different Greek words for "love:" agape, storge, phileo, and eros.

While the agape love of God is the unconditional love that God has for us, and we strive to love with this kind of love, it would be insufficient to say: "I *love* God like I *love* pizza." In the same way, the meaning of some of these Hebrew words for praise gets diluted.

One of these 7 Hebrew words is "Towdah." It means, "A confession. A sacrifice of praise. Thanksgiving for things not yet received." Sometimes it's easy to break out in a song of praise and worship when everything is going well. It's a different story when our emotions have us down, when circumstances are painful and feel uncertain. This is when it is truly a "sacrifice of praise."

It's like when Paul and Silas were beaten, imprisoned, and in chains. What did they do? They sang. They didn't sulk. We could easily understand if they just laid there and cried, but instead they praised God with "expectant praise." This is "Towdah!" They sang songs of deliverance *before* they were actually delivered!

No matter what you are facing or experiencing, you are invited to Towdah God and sing praises of confession, of expectation, and of breakthrough.

> "All you saints! Sing your hearts out to God! Thank him to his face! He gets angry once in a while, but across a lifetime there is only love. The nights of crying your eyes out give way to days of laughter."
>
> Psalm 30:4 -5 MSG

Prayer

I praise You and I worship You today, God. Thank You that I have been set free. Thank You that You are Jehovah Nissi: the God who redeems my life from destruction. I receive Your Word that "It is finished" and that I overcome by the blood of the lamb and the word of my testimony. Thank You for victory. Thank You that You are undefeated, and I am under Your wings. Whatever I'm facing, You have the final say, and in the end, I have victorious breakthrough. I will sing it. I will declare it.

In the mighty Name of Jesus, Amen!

Future Rulers of The World

There shall be no night there:
They need no lamp nor light of
the sun, for the Lord God gives
them light. And <u>they shall reign</u>
forever and ever.

Revelation 22:5 NKJV

Message

Look at the first chapter of the first book of the Bible:

> And God blessed them. And God said to them, "Be fruitful and multiply and fill the earth and **subdue it, and have dominion** over the fish of the sea and over the birds of the heavens and over every living thing that moves on the earth.
>
> Genesis 1:28 ESV

Then look at the last chapter of the last book:

> There shall be no night there: They need no lamp nor light of the sun, for the Lord God gives them light. And **they shall reign** forever and ever.
>
> Revelation 22:5 NKJV

Do you see the connection? Do you see what God is doing? He is restoring mankind's authority and dominion! In the creation narrative, He put Adam and Eve in the garden to rule it. In John's Revelation of the new world to come, God's people will rule and reign with Christ, submitted to Him. As my friend, Christian Santiago says it, "we were born to rule." What a beautiful mysterious truth it is that we are the future rulers of the world!

And it's not only these couple of scriptures that speak to this. It's actually all throughout the Bible. Once you see it, you can't unsee it!

If we endure, **We shall also reign** with Him. If we deny Him, He also will deny us.

II Timothy 2:12 NKJV

and has made us **kings and priests** to His God and Father, to Him be glory and dominion forever and ever. Amen.

Revelation 1:6 NKJV

To him who overcomes I will grant to **sit with Me on My throne**, as I also overcame and sat down with My Father on His throne.

Revelation 3:21 NKJV

And have made us kings and priests to our God; And **we shall reign** on the earth.

Revelation 5:10 NKJV

Look at this beautiful prophecy in Amos:

"Behold, the days are coming," declares the Lord, "when the plowman shall overtake the reaper and the treader of grapes him who sows the seed; the mountains shall drip sweet wine, and all the hills shall flow with it. I will restore the fortunes of my people Israel, and they shall **rebuild the ruined cities** and inhabit them; they shall plant vineyards and drink their wine, and they shall **make gardens and eat their fruit.** I will plant them on their land, and they shall never again be

uprooted out of the land that I have given them,"
says the Lord your God.

Amos 9:13-15 ESV

We will "make gardens and eat their fruit." That's *Garden of Eden* language! We will "rebuild ruined cities and inhabit them." That's *New World* language! And if our prayer is that God's Kingdom would come and His will would be done on Earth as it is in Heaven through us, then we ought to live into this reality now! The Holy Spirit empowers us to live as the sons and daughters of God, as royalty, as rulers with God-given authority!

This has implications for how we live, how we act, how we solve problems, how we create, how we make art, how we inspire, and how we love! Let us live in the reality today that we are the future rulers of the coming new world, reigning with Christ, and in glad submission to Him.

Prayer

God, I'm in awe that You would give me the honor and privilege of ruling and reigning with You. Thank You for creating me and bestowing on me that kind of honor and glory. Help me to live worthy of this glorious truth. Give me confidence and wisdom to live like the ruler over my life and the areas of influence that You have blessed me with.

I humbly submit to You, Lord, and with Your authority, I take dominion over every part of my heart, soul, and mind.

I take authority over the enemy and all evil spirits, as they are under my feet.

I take authority over temptation, as Your Word is truth and life.

I take authority over my finances, as You have given me dominion over them, and I am blessed and highly favored to generate wealth and to be radically generous.

I take authority over my schedule, as You have given me a sound mind to not be mastered by anything, to but to make my schedule work for me.

I take authority to be creative, and to let the creativity of Heaven flow through me and into the world.

In the mighty name of Jesus Christ, Amen.

Rulers & Refugees

Dear friends, I urge you, as foreigners and exiles, to abstain from sinful desires, which wage war against your soul.

1 Peter 2:11 NIV

Message

Wait! What? I thought we were rulers. I thought we were the future rulers of the world?! We still are. But we're foreigners and exiles too.

Just like God's people were exiled from Jerusalem into Babylonian captivity around 607 B.C., we too are the chosen people of God in a land that is not as it is supposed to be, currently in a fallen state. God's plan is to redeem all things. His plan is to bring the New Heavens and the New Earth down to this world as we know it, and reset it perfectly and completely. He will restore it similarly to how He created it in the Garden of Eden in the beginning.

But in the meantime, we are actively acting as ambassadors for God, bringing the love of God, the truth of God, and the Kingdom of God to the world in its current fallen state. And as the chosen people of God, we won't always be "cool." We won't always be "popular." In fact, I like the way the King James Version puts it just two verses before our verse above:

> "But ye are a chosen generation, a royal priesthood, an holy nation, a **peculiar people**; that ye should shew forth the praises of him who hath called you out of darkness into his marvellous light:"
>
> 1 Peter 2:9 KJV

Wow! So yes, we are created in the image of God, created to rule and reign with Christ (2 Timothy 2:12), and to sit with Him on His throne (Revelation 3:21), but we are *also* "foreigners," "exiles," and "peculiar people."

My encouragement to you is to *own your weirdness*. You're not supposed to be cool. You're not supposed to be popular. You're supposed to be bringing the Kingdom of God, preparing to rule and reign with Him forever, and to endure the hardships of living as a foreigner and exile in a fallen world.

As the prophet Jeremiah said, the way the people of God ought to live as exiles in Babylon was not to rebel, but to seek its well being and remain faithful to God throughout the whole experience. So we seek the world's well being, endure suffering, and remain faithful to God to shield us and protect us for our good and His glory in a world that is waiting to be perfectly redeemed.

Prayer

Jesus, I need Your strength. Holy Spirit, I need Your power. I know who I am and I know Whose I am, but life isn't always easy. Empower me to not feel like I always need to "fit in." Empower me to endure suffering in a way that glorifies You. Help me keep my eyes on You and on the coming Kingdom and the renewal of all things. Give me tastes of it today and every day, even in this fallen world, to keep me going. Thank You God. I receive it now.

Amen.

Think BIGGER

Now to Him who is able to do exceedingly abundantly above all that we ask or think, according to the power that works in us, to Him be glory in the church by Christ Jesus to all generations, forever and ever. Amen.

Ephesians 3:20 -21 NKJV

Message

For whatever magnificence you've experienced of God, there is more. He's the God of the impossible. He's the God who created the Heavens and the Earth by literally just speaking them into existence. This is the same God who promises to meet every single one of our needs (Philippians 4:19).

What dreams or breakthroughs have entered into your mind that you've been unsure of? What doubts do you have about what can be accomplished in you and through you? If the scripture says that He who is joined to the Lord is one spirit with Him (1 Corinthians 6:17), then His power is accessible and even made manifest through our own lives. What did Ephesians 3:20 say about His power? "the power that works *in us!*"

Don't limit God and don't limit yourself if you are one with Him. He is the God of the impossible and He loves to do unimaginable things through the lowliest, most unsuspecting people. This should encourage you to take risks. This should motivate you to not shrink back in fear, but make the most of every opportunity with a Godly confidence. No matter how big you can dream, what's in the mind of God is still infinitely bigger than what you're thinking.

And when things don't go according to plan or maybe you experience disappointment, you can be sure that there is more opportunity coming up ahead, and plenty more abundance in store from your Heavenly Father.

The truth is that we live out what we believe most deeply. We literally think, act, and operate in such a way so that we ultimately manifest whatever set of beliefs that we hold in our hearts. If you believe that you'll never have enough resources, you'll never give generously and you'll never take the appropriate steps of confidence to earn more, or master a skill that can lead you to greater financial increase. But if you believe that God has abundance in store for you, you will give more lavishly and operate with a zeal and God-confidence that He can and wants to provide you with infinitely more than you could ever imagine!

Make no mistake, this is all about His glory and expanding His Kingdom. It's not about us having material wealth that will be here and gone tomorrow. But it's a beautiful thing how He brings glory to Himself and expands His Kingdom through us! When we operate with a humble yet holy confidence, it is what I think Saint Ireneaus was talking about when he said, "The glory of God is man fully alive."

Believe God that He is able *and will do* exceedingly and abundantly above what you could ask or think *through you!* You are invited into this beautiful truth. Get it deep inside your being so that you can live it out with your life.

Prayer

God of exceeding abundance, align my heart and mind with Yours. I want to live in a way that brings Your Kingdom here on Earth. I'm asking you to expand my mindset and help me to believe in the deepest parts of me that You have much more in store. I renounce the lies of the enemy that I will never have enough, that I'll always be stuck right where I'm at, or that You don't want more for me. That is a limiting belief that I want to lay at Your feet and let You annihilate. I want to bring You glory! I want to expand Your Kingdom! But help me to first better understand Your Kingdom. Open my eyes, Lord. Thank You.

Amen.

Index

An index of verses referenced in each chapter.

DAY THREE
It Gets Better

Psalm 30:5b

DAY FOUR
Towdah (Expectant Praise)

DAY FIVE
Future Rulers of The World

DAY SIX
Rulers & Refugees

DAY SEVEN
Think BIGGER